The Art of Gift Wrapping

The Art of Gift Wrapping

by Jane Cornell

Introduction by Roger Horchow

THE WARNER LIFESTYLE LIBRARY

WARNER BOOKS

A Warner Communications Company

THE WARNER LIFESTYLE LIBRARY

 Created by Media Projects Incorporated

Photography by Sally Andersen-Bruce
Illustrations by Gabriel Casuso

Staff, Media Projects Incorporated
Carter Smith: President
Beverly Gary Kempton: Senior Editor
Bryan Dew: Designer
Ellen Coffey: Editorial Assistant

Contributing Editor: Jane Randolph Cary
Copy Editing: Evie Righter

Warner Books, Inc., 75 Rockefeller Plaza, New York, N.Y. 10019

 A Warner Communications Company

Printed in the United States of America
First Printing: October 1980
10 9 8 7 6 5 4 3 2 1

Library of Congress Cataloging in Publication Data

Cornell, Jane.
   The art of gift wrapping.

   Includes index.
   1. Gift wrapping. I. Title.
TT870.C67   745.54   80-14156
ISBN 0-446-51212-5 (hardcover)
ISBN 0-446-97474-9 (U.S. pbk.)
ISBN 0-446-97769-1 (Canadian pbk.)

Also in The Warner Lifestyle Library
The Art of Table Decoration

Contents

Introduction

You might consider that the manner of giving is often worth more than the gift itself — or at least as much.

We know that the most treasured gift frequently has little to do with its price and much to do with the thoughtfulness that went into its choice. The special quality of the selection. Remembering a favorite interest. Adding to a cherished collection. However, we may tend to neglect what the gift's wrapping says, the tone it sets. The presentation is really our first message. Even though the wrapping deliberately hides the gift, we show our affection through the care we've taken to cover and adorn it.

The wrapping may be lavish or simple. That's not important. Materials can be bought or made, and they can be expensive or cost very little. It doesn't really matter. It is the imagination and the spirit we bring to wrapping a present that make it fun for us to do and especially fun to receive.

The Art of Gift Wrapping will tell you all you need to know to breathe life into that plain container you are planning to use: how to wrap different shapes; materials to buy or make, and how best to make them work for your needs; how to coordinate colors, patterns, textures; how to form a classic bow and tie a basic knot; how to piece with paper; make bags from fabric remnants; and even, in case you've wondered, how to wrap an umbrella.

It offers hundreds of hints, suggestions, and step-by-step descriptions of ways to enhance a package, and inventive garnishes to use. Stars and glitter hardly come as a surprise on the outside of a package, but who would expect a piece of pasta? For trimmings, you can raid the icebox, the desk, the storage closet, the garden, or your secret treasure chest.

Because the act of giving is such a personal one, this book encourages you to think of themes particularly suited to the one who is to receive the gift, and it offers any number of ideas and instructions on how to carry them out. You can decorate the gift to look like something it is not, or wrap it to highlight and actually give away its contents. Whether it is how to wrap a parcel for mailing, how to cover such a dainty object as a bicycle, or how to marbelize paper, you'll find it here.

Art is human creativity, and gift wrapping can be a creative act for you—a wonderful means of self-expression. Undoubtedly countless ideas of your own will come to mind once you have tried your hand at these in the enchanting *Art of Gift Wrapping*.

Roger Horchow

Roger Horchow
President, The Horchow Collection

Yes, there are dozens of wrapping techniques to make your package look beautiful. But there are just two basic shapes, and knowing how to cover them is where it all begins. It is amazing how dissimilar the same shape can look when it appears in a variety of sizes and proportions. The matchbox and piano crate are both cubes, and the method of wrapping either is much the same.

The other category of basic shapes is cylinders and spheres, and they too range from the minuscule to the vast. Then there are the amorphous objects — the snow shovel or the piece of modern sculpture. They need not dismay you. Decide which shape they most closely approximate (cubic or cylindrical) and wrap them accordingly.

The basic shape is easy to determine once you develop the knack. And do not be intimidated by the outsized. Most major household appliances, for instance, are cubes. True, you will certainly have to piece the paper to wrap a washing machine, but the technique is akin to the one you would use for a handkerchief box. On the other hand, a new pair of skis, a seemingly hopeless form to enclose, resembles a long cylinder and can be handsomely wrapped by adapting one of the cylindrical techniques.

The same principle applies to the very small package. A powder box is a short cylinder. And while the ring box might harbor gold and the Crackerjack box merely tin, when their outsides are to be wrapped, they stand as equals — two cubes.

Opposite: Almost all gifts lend themselves to one of the two basic wrapping shapes: the cube and its variations, or the cylinder and its variations.

Squares and Rectangles

The basic cube or box shapes. Once you learn how to properly wrap one rectangle, you will be able to tackle any other — a tie box or boot box, little or large.

Measuring

Measuring paper accurately saves time and money. Money, because you use paper efficiently and waste less. Time, because it is easier to work with paper if it is the right size. The sides and ends of wrapping paper form perfect right angles, so use them in cutting paper to size. The truer the angles, the simpler it is to line up the paper and box. Here are some pointers:

1. To find out if the width of the paper that you have will fit the package, put one side of the box at the edge of the paper, flop the box over to the next side, then to the third side, and finally to the last side. Make sure you have allowed for all 4 sides. Add an additional 1 inch for folding under a hem and overlapping.

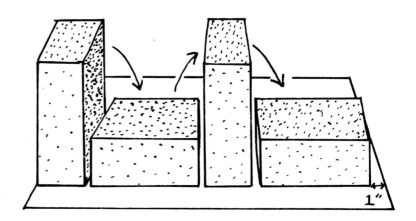

Flop the box on all 4 sides, add 1 inch, and you have the width for the wrapping paper.

Wrap the paper around the box. Center the seam on the back of the box and secure. Place tape on the paper and pull the paper taut around the box. Tape the center seam, then each end.

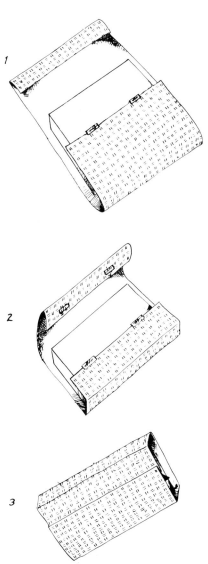

2. To find out if you have enough paper to cover the ends of a deep box: Allow an extra amount of paper — at least half the depth of the box at each end. For flat boxes, simply be sure that the ends of the paper are long enough to fold over the back of the box, allowing at least 1 inch.

3. You can also use a piece of string to measure the length and width. Knot one end of the string and, to determine the width, hold the string at one side of the box, and wrap it around the box. Grasp it where the string meets the knot. Stretch the string across the paper and add 1 inch for overlapping. To determine the length of paper you need, stretch the string down one side of the box, across the length of the box, and up the other side of the box.

Taping Techniques

Nothing spoils the effect of a beautiful package more than a messy job of taping. You need tape to get crisp lines and to hold the paper taut. Bulges and wrinkles never enhance.

Transparent tape that is adhesive on both sides — called double-stick tape — allows you to keep this homely tool hidden to the eye. It helps produce a neater, prettier package and thus is the first choice. The second choice is transparent tape, preferably non-reflecting, which is adhesive on one side only.

1. Begin by taping the center back seam. Turn under a ½-inch hem at the top of the paper so that no raw edges show. Tape the lower edge to the box, or just hold it firmly in place.

2. Place double-stick tape on the inside of the top ½-inch hem.

3. Press the top paper into place.

If you are using single-sided transparent tape, press it on the inside of the top hem and then double the tape, adhesive side out. Now press the top paper into place. The tape will not show. Use it the same way when you tape the final flap of the package ends.

Folding and Mitering Corners

Ends show. The trimmer they are, the trimmer the overall look of the package. Some people fold the sides in first and then fold over the top and bottom flaps, while others fold down the top flap and then fold in the sides. Whichever way you choose, learn to fit the paper snugly around the ends of the package and to make clean, sharp, straight folds. Here are instructions for the latter method:

1. Center the box on the paper.

2. From the back at one end fold down the top flap and finger-crease the edge. Press the paper into the corners to create right angles at each side and finger-press the folds at the edges of the angles.

3. Fold both sides toward the center, making sure the paper fits closely along the box edge. Secure the sides with tape placed horizontally and toward the center of the box so that it will not be seen when the final flap is folded. Fold over about ½ inch of the raw edge of the final flap and finger-crease it straight across.

4. Carefully fold the final flap up. Finger-press the fold to be certain it fits. Then, release the fold and flap. Place double-stick tape on the inside of the final flap, draw the flap up, and press. Repeat for the opposite end.

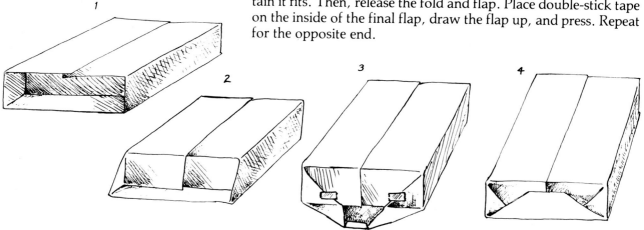

Center the box on the paper. Fold down the top flap. Fold the corners in snugly and fold over the raw edges of the flap. Fold up the final flap and secure.

Cylinders and Spheres

A tobacco tin is short and squat; a baseball bat, long and club-like. And there is little doubt that a basketball is a sphere. No matter. They are all wrapped in a similar fashion — as cylinders. In each case, to measure the paper you need you must first determine the circumference of the package. Then allow enough paper to finish the ends with whatever design you choose.

Snapper Wrap

It really is not as hard as it sounds. In fact it is as easy as it is basic. Much as in the child's party favor, each end is decorative, either fringed or solid. Consider crepe paper for some snapper wraps, and flute the ends into floral shapes. Or use layers of tissue paper and fringe the ends. With a little help, youngsters can quickly learn this technique and use it for the packages they wrap.

1. Cut the paper the circumference of the cylinder and add 1 inch for folding back a hem at the raw edge and for overlapping. For length, cut the paper at least 1½ times the diameter of the cylinder.

2. Center the cylinder on the paper. Make sure when positioning the cylinder that there is surplus paper at either end. Wrap the paper around the cylinder and secure the paper along the seam to the ends.

3. Gather in each end, pinching the paper together. Add a ribbon, tie, or decorative tape, then fluff the ends from the inside to make them appear full and, if necessary, trim them so that they are in proportion to the cylinder.

4. For a more fanciful look, flatten the ends and cut them with scissors to create streamers. If you are using a layer of tissue paper in one color, add an extra layer in a different color and you will have two-colored streamers — festive and fun.

With pretty reversible paper, gather the ends and turn them inside out. Tape the newly exposed paper into place in a softened mushroom shape.

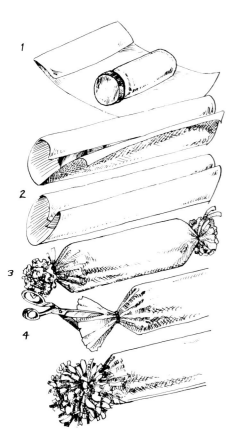

Measure the paper. Secure the paper around the centered cylinder. Bunch the ends. Secure and fluff. Or cut the ends to create streamers.

Accordion Fold Ends

This style of wrapping is particularly useful when you want the finished cylinder to stand up, as the folds at the bottom of the container are relatively flat. The sleekness of the top folds gives a streamlined look to the entire package. If you wish, embellish the top with a bow, pom-pom, or your gift tag.

Tissue paper is excellent for this treatment, as is crepe paper. You can stretch the crepe paper around the circumference of the package and leave it unstretched at the ends. Other lightweight and pliant wrapping papers also work well with accordion fold ends. The only papers to avoid are extremely stiff ones, which make folding difficult.

To finish off the top end and cover its center, you might fashion a medallion from one of the motifs of the paper, or use a self-stick seal to match the paper.

1. Cut the paper the circumference of the cylinder and add 1 inch for folding back a hem at the raw edge and for overlapping. For length, add just a little over half of the diameter of the cylinder at each end.

2. Center the cylinder on the paper. Make sure when positioning the cylinder that there is surplus paper at either end. Wrap the paper around the cylinder and secure it along the seam to the ends.

3. Beginning at the overlapping seam, fold in one end by pressing paper in toward the center. Rotate the cylinder in your hand as you do so and continue to make even pleats.

4. Secure the folds at the center of the top with transparent tape, preferably double-stick.

5. Press the last fold into position, release, and turn under the raw edge. Anchor it with double-stick tape if you are leaving it unadorned. If you plan to decorate the end, just secure the final fold with tape.

Go back over the folds and press them down as needed to make the edge of the cylinder appear smooth. Repeat for the opposite end.

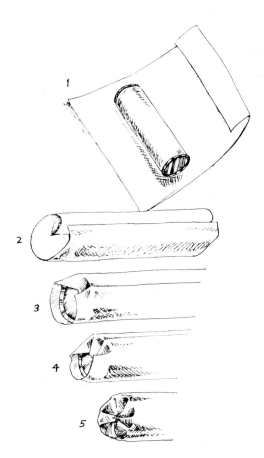

Cut the paper wide enough to surround the cylinder and add half the diameter of the cylinder at each end. Tape the paper around the cylinder. Start at the overlap to fold end paper in. Overlap and tape the folds, rotating the cylinder.

Roll the cylinder from the corner until the paper overlaps by half the cylinder's diameter. Add 1 inch. Cut the paper diagonally. Roll the cylinder in the paper from the long edge to the "point." Tape the points on the cylinder and bunch the ends. Flair the ends, or bunch them into mushroom shape, and tape.

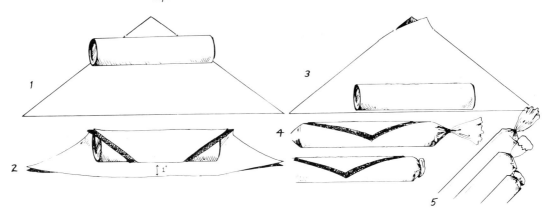

The Croissant Wrap

1. To detetermine where to cut the paper, place 2 pre-cut sheets of paper, in contrasting colors, on a table, with the sheet to be on the inside of the wrap on top of the sheet to be on the outside. Position a corner of the top sheet about ½ inch from the corresponding corner of the bottom sheet. Place the cylinder on the paper.

2. Roll the cylinder directly in from the corner, wrapping the paper around it. (When rolled, the paper will overlap the ends of the cylinder by half the cylinder's diameter.) Now add 1 inch (see Figure #2), and cut the paper diagonally.

3. Unroll the cylinder. The paper on top will be a large triangular shape; the sheet beneath, smaller. Center the cylinder and roll it up in the paper, starting from the longest side and moving to the "point" across from it. (If necessary, anchor the paper by taping it to the cylinder.)

4. Secure the points of the triangle with double-stick tape positioned under the paper, or with a medallion or seal.

5. Trim and tie the ends, flair the ends, crush them into pompoms, or bunch them into mushroom shapes and tape.

15

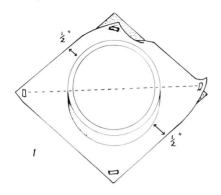

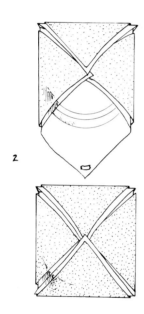

Place the container in the center of a paper square. Fold over one end and both sides and tape. Fold over last end and tape.

The Egg Roll Wrap

This wrap is splendid for flat shapes in particular, which is why it is also called the envelope fold. Use one or two sheets of paper. If you use two, make the outside paper smaller than the inside one, thus ensuring that the inside paper will be visible.

1. To measure the paper, place the container, such as a box, kitty-cornered on the paper. Make certain the paper will fold up and over the container by at least ½ inch.
Draw an imaginary line through the center of the container. Where it meets the edge of the paper, cut the paper to make a square.
If you are using 2 papers, trim the outer piece so that equal borders will show on all 4 sides. Place the smaller sheet on the table and center the larger sheet over it. Place container diagonally in the middle.

2. Fold up one end and secure it with tape. Next, fold up one side, then the other, envelope style, and secure them with tape.

3. Fold up the last end and secure. Add a medallion or gift tag in the center.

Permanent Covers

No longer waste for the trash basket, used boxes embellished with permanent covers are a unique way of giving two presents at one time. Most of us use boxes in which to store things. How nice to receive one so handsomely decorated that it is not consigned to an instant back-shelf life. When selecting a covering, find a paper sturdy enough to last. Also, high-gloss paper shuns more dust than a matte-finished one. Consider as well self-stick paper, self-stick plastic, or self-stick vinyl, most of which have built-in soil resistance. Take special care to neatly finish the seams and folds.

Opposite: The charm of a covered hatbox ensures it a permanent place in the closet. Self-stick paper dresses up this one.

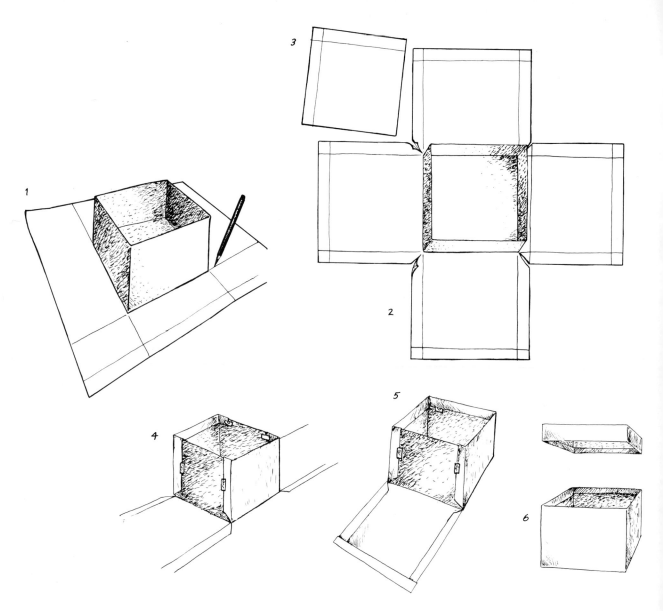

Trace around the box base and extend the lines to form a square. Draw 1-inch flaps on each side of the cross, mitered into the corners. Cut around the cross leaving 1 inch for flaps on each side. Wrap 2 opposite sides up, over, and into the box. Secure the flaps with tape. Fold up the remaining flaps and tape. Repeat the process for the lid.

Covering a Square or Rectangular Box

Any number of square or rectangular boxes lend themselves to permanent covers. If you have a box with a lid that extends to the base of the box, you only have to cover the lid to achieve an effect.

Boxes with lids covering only part of the sides of the box may double your work, but here is your chance to be super-creative. Match the lid and bottom, or combine patterns for a mix-match look. A solid bottom with a printed lid is an attractive combination. Another is reversible paper — one side on the bottom, its reverse on the top. Imagine paper with red hearts on a white background for the lid and white hearts on a red background for the bottom. Some gift paper manufacturers offer such coordinates, or you can invent your own. Whichever you do, here's how to do it:

1. Place the box in the center of a pre-cut piece of paper and trace around its base. Measure the height of one side of the box's bottom (i.e., lower container), and add at least 1 inch. Extend all 4 lines that distance, thus creating a square with a cross in it.

2. Draw 1-inch flaps on each side of the cross, mitered into the corners.

3. Cut out around the flaps, and into the miter, on all 4 sides.

4. Wrap 2 opposite sides up, over, and into the box. These flaps will overlap onto the ends of the box both inside and out. Secure the flaps with tape inside and out.

5. Bring the 2 remaining sides up, and anchor, if necessary, by putting double-stick tape along the turned-in flap sides.

Pull the flaps over and into the box and anchor them inside. Make sure all sides fit snugly, as the lid must be able to slide down over the paper.

To cover the lid, repeat the process.

To line the lid and bottom of the box, use the same technique, but reverse it. There is one change: Bring the lining just short of the top edge of the bottom and just short of the rim of the lid, thus ensuring that the lid and bottom fit snugly. (Turn under the lining's raw edges.)

Cut paper larger than the lid to cover the lid. Adhere the paper to the top, and trim to just cover the sides. Slit and adhere the paper to the sides. Adhere a strip of paper around the side of the lid. Fold and adhere the paper to the inside of the rim.

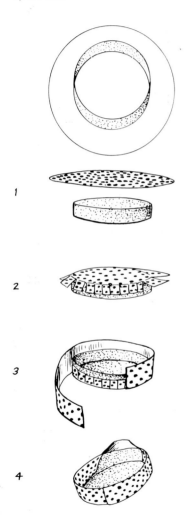

Covering a Round Box

Round boxes have a romance all their own. Hats may or may not be in vogue, but their boxes remain with us as a lovely bit of nostalgia. Bedeck an old one, or buy a new one to cover with fabulous paper. A word to the wise: Choose paper that is not difficult to match up and align, as the varying planes of a round box make matching almost impossible. Don't be deterred. Covering a round box is not an arduous task. By far the simplest way is with self-stick paper, but you can follow these same instructions using almost any paper, and white all-purpose glue or spray-on adhesive.

1. To cover the lid of a round box, cut the paper large enough to cover the lid and its sides, and adhere it to the top surface only.

2. Cut slits or wedges in the paper so that it overlaps on the sides. (Trim paper before slitting, if necessary.) Adhere the paper to the sides of the lid. (If you are using glue, allow it to dry completely.) Make sure no paper overlaps the bottom edge of the lid.

3. Measure a piece of paper the circumference of the lid and add ½ inch for overlapping. Cut the paper. Make it as wide as the depth of the lid and add at least an additional ½ inch to turn. Line up one edge of the paper just below the top of the lid and adhere the paper, circling the lid.

4. Fold the paper over the rim and adhere it inside the lid.

5. For the round box itself, cut the paper long enough to encircle the box plus a ½-inch overlap. Allow at least a ½-inch overlap at the top and a 1-inch overlap at the base. For larger boxes, allow more on both ends of the paper.

6. Center the paper to provide correct overlaps at the base and top, and adhere the paper to the sides of the box. Fold the paper over the top of the rim (as in Step #4 of lid instruction illustration) and adhere it.

7. Cut slits or wedges in the paper extending below the base of the box. Adhere the slit paper to the underside. For a professional finish, cover the underside with paper cut to fit.

Opposite: You can easily buy such beautiful bags, or go all out and make your own.

Making Paper Bags

Colorful and ornamental paper bags are the least involved wrapping for some presents. Nestle the gift, for example, in a safe bed of tissue and let some of the paper peak above the bag's upper edge.

Making your own bag is a somewhat complicated procedure, but do not be put off. Once you have shaped the first, others will not appear nearly as formidable. Basically, it involves constructing a tube of paper, folding it to form the bottom, and finishing the upper edge.

Before measuring the paper — rag paper is strong and particularly good for bags — decide how deep and wide you want the bag to be. It can be large or small, but in the interests of clarity let us imagine one 2 inches deep by 4 inches wide. Now add $\frac{1}{2}$ inch to the figure: 2 sides $(2 + 2 = 4)$ + the back and front $(4 + 4 = 8)$ + $\frac{1}{2}$ inch $= 12\frac{1}{2}$ inches. Measure the paper $12\frac{1}{2}$ inches wide.

Make the bag as tall as you wish, but add 2 inches at the top plus half the width of one side. If our bag is to be 6 inches tall, it is 6 inches + 2 inches + 1 inch $= 9$ inches. Measure the paper 9 inches long.

1. Fold paper in $\frac{1}{2}$ inch along one side. Overlap the other edge with it to make a roll shape. Glue securely with white all-purpose glue and allow it to dry. Fold the paper flat and crease the opposite side (fold A).

2. Starting at the glued edge, measure off the distance of the depth of the bag (in this case 2 inches). Crease paper along this line and line up the new crease with the glued edge (fold B).

3. Crease the inside fold of the side section (fold C).
Repeat the process on the opposite side of the bag (A). Measure the depth (2 inches), crease and tuck in the side section (fold D), and crease the back corner down the side.

4. To make the bottom, fold the bottom edge of the bag up half the width of one of its sides (1 inch in our example). Fold the 4 corners into 45-degree triangles.

5. Open up the bag and turn the folded section to the inside. Fold in the sides first. (The triangle folds make this step easier).

Cut a cardboard rectangle the exact size of the bag's bottom and insert it. Glue the side flaps to the cardboard, or tape with transparent tape.

6. Fold the front and back flaps over the bottom, glue and seal them with a separate piece of paper to cover any gap, and as reinforcement.

7. To make the handles, cut the paper as long as you want plus 4 times the handle's width.

8. Fold the strip and glue it.

9. Slit holes where the handles go into the bag.

10. Fold down the top of the bag (2 inches). Open the fold, insert the handles, refold, and glue the handles and the top fold at the same time.

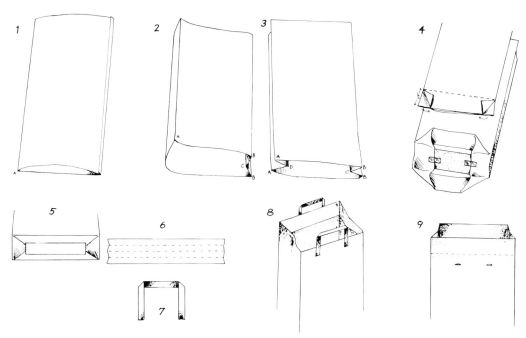

To make your own bags, follow the steps in the text. Be sure to use strong paper.

Almost as important as the choice of a gift is the paper in which to wrap it. Today the variety of papers is infinite — an impressive array of weights, textures, finishes, colors, and patterns. Add to this the papers you can make yourself, and the possibilities are as rich as your imagination.

A word about selecting papers. Aside from their visual aspects, consider their individual characteristics and the job you have at hand. While a certain pattern might be glorious, the paper's weight could make it totally unsuitable for your specific need. Alas, the marriage of tissue paper and a hammer is not a happy one. Here then are some types of paper you will encounter:

Crepe and tissue paper. These are best for bulky and free-form items, and are generally easy for children to handle. Tissue paper can be inexpensive — patterned ones tend to be more costly — but remember when you are deciding whether or not to buy that you will want double thickness.

Metallic and super-glossy paper. Dramatic as they are, they do not suffer mistakes lightly. Reserve them for easy-to-wrap presents.

Patterned papers. There are, of course, exceptions, but generally small prints look best on small boxes and large prints on large boxes. Do make sure that at least one complete motif shows on the front of the package — one of the purposes of a pattern, after all.

Thin versus heavy paper. Thin paper is fine as long as the gift it encloses does not show through. However, heavy paper tends to look more expensive.

Opposite: Reversible paper can perform double duty, and double the fun.

Papers for Kids

Rare is the child not enchanted with the idea of presents. The buried treasure, of course, is the prize, but its wrapping can hint of the good things in store. Wrappings need not be elaborate. Search your childhood to find themes and personalize the wrapping as much as possible.

Age determines the complexity of the wrapping. Keep presents for toddlers easy to open and use little tape or none at all. If you do use it, make sure it can be ripped off without too much effort. Tie bows that can be quickly undone. In other words, minimize frustration.

Colors for children include the primaries (red, yellow, blue), or any other bright color. Wrapping the present in the child's favorite hue is thoughtful, and exciting for the youngster.

Themes range from favorite toys to current folk heroes — Superman, the Peanuts gang, or other cartoon characters. Avoid the more sophisticated or subtle motif unless you know the young recipient has such a passion.

Wrappings that are too luxurious often promise more than the gift delivers. Try not to raise a child's expectations to unrealistic levels. If the present is a simple pair of socks, do not put it in a wrap befitting a baseball glove.

Wrappings that hint of what is inside are fun for children. A new pair of running shoes, for instance, could be wrapped in paper with a motif of sports equipment. If the present is a ball, you will give the game away when the wrapping conforms to the ball's shape.

Opposite: A "surprise" ball promises even more surprise when it is festooned with tissue-wrapped extras.

Papers that are Tailored

Tailored wrappings are particularly appropriate for men's gifts, and for general social gift-giving. It would be fitting to cover a gift for an office colleague with a tailored paper, for instance; an ornate wrap would be an overstatement. Then too, there are times you simply want a crisp, uncluttered look. Some tips:

Patterns frequently used to these ends include almost all the geometrics—stripes, polka dots, plaids, men's tie designs, even supergraphic geometrics.

Colors are generally muted, though, with such shades as brown, gray, cocoa, white, navy, and black dominant. In truth, just about any color, even bright ones, can be used for tailored packages. Add a smart ribbon, or ties, and a wonderfully individualistic style can be created with the simplest of solid wraps. And do not overlook the more humble brown kraft papers, understated enough to make them ideal backgrounds for casual gifts. You can keep the wrapping plain with jute-type ties or dress it up with plaid or checked ribbons in varying tones of brown.

Wrapping with geometrics calls for more care than wrapping with papers that have no obvious lines or repeats. Ideally, stripes and plaids should line up with the box edges. When the patterns are out of line, the whole box takes on an awkward and distorted look. Because matching of edges and patterns is important, do not use geometrics on boxes that are not true rectangles or cylinders. And once you start wrapping, take the time to line up the folds and flaps at the ends so that the change in pattern direction is even and pleasing to the eye. The tailored package is most attractive when the pattern lends proportion to it visually — vertical stripes running crosswise on a long, thin box, for example.

Opposite: tailored wrappings. Trim, handsome, and a good choice for men.

Papers That Are Romantic

Our response to wrapping paper often mirrors our personality. Perhaps at heart you are a romantic, or suspect the same of someone else. Whatever the reason, romantic presents are a joy to wrap. Be as fanciful and extravagant as you like. Or, if the sentimental appeals, *be* sentimental, for this is the time and the place to let fantasy reign.

Romantic colors include the pastels, as soft and gentle as an English garden at sunset. Lacy white-on-white wrappings, or those embellished with gold and silver, also convey romance. If the theatrical is what you seek, try such regal shades as violet, ruby red, or jade green. They are reminiscent of a romantic Victorian valentine.

The traditional themes on romantic paper are hearts and flowers, hand-me-downs from the wrappings of the late 19th century. And if it is not hearts, you can be sure it will be flowers. Whether in a realistic rendering or in a stylized one, flowers are in perennial bloom on romantic papers. Next in popularity are motifs of such genteel pursuits as embroidery, stitchery, or quilting. Finally, some papers rely simply on color to have their romantic say. Almost anything pink falls into this category; there are even those who would include Miss Piggy.

Be they presents for teen-aged girls, who especially love romantic papers, or their elders, the gift itself should be as romantic as its wrapping. Pink paper with white hearts is a poor choice for a new dishwasher and an even poorer one for the encyclopedia, unless, of course, each happens to be given at a bridal shower, that clarion call for romantic wrappings. Other such obvious occasions are anniversaries, weddings, and Valentine's Day. Then there are those times special only to the two of you. They, perhaps, are the most romantic of all.

Opposite: Say it with carnations on dusty rose paper crowned with a luxurious bow.

Papers Out of the Ordinary

Everyone has a friend whose tastes are a bit esoteric, if not downright wacky. Finding a suitable wrapping paper for that person can be great sport. You can be as eccentric as you wish, knowing that both the package and your efforts will be truly appreciated.

It may be your own style to set trends or to fashion packages into distinctive works of art. In either case, a wide variety of spectacular papers is available. All may not please you, but you will want to try some, at least once. Here are a few suggestions for finding those out-of-the-ordinary papers:

Trend-setting patterns. Today's hit movies, current home furnishings ideas, fads, and the newest look in gift cards are often reflected in gift wrappings. A science fiction movie, or a revival of the sleek look of the '30s, '40s, even '50s can spark entire new lines in gift paper. Pop art and super-graphics have been inspirations for dynamic papers. It is easy to identify a trend-setting paper; it echoes the latest motifs in accessories, as well as your interests and those of your friends.

Sophisticated patterns. Sophistication is a word that almost defies definition; some wrapping papers just *are* more sophisticated than others. Some may blend unusual and offbeat colors, often muted, in a novel way—a series of browns with gold perhaps. Others will be vivid and theatrical—black accented with sharp contrasts.

Truly expensive papers. They reflect the extra work put into them. Silk-screened and hand-marbelized papers are examples. Then too, a sophisticated pattern is often printed on good paper, thus raising its cost.

Opposite: Out-of-the-ordinary packages are often wrapped in time-honored motifs, rendered in a subtle blending of colors.

Special Occasion Wrappings

It may be a suddenly remembered birthday or an anniversary. Whatever the event, you are certain to find a wrapping paper designed for just that special occasion. As most gifts are given to celebrate such moments, the selection of gift paper is often very large. Here are several ideas for themes. If you do not find them incorporated in the paper's design, look for trims to tell the story.

Birthdays. Paper with the theme of a person's hobby, craft, or job is one thought. Or paper in the color of their birthstone, or printed with the flower of their birthday month. Numbers also work, even for those who have long since stopped at age thirty-nine. Or make the wrapping a clue. Wrap a blue-and-white-striped paper around a man's shirt box and with a felt-tip marker draw a collar, some buttons, and a pocket on it. If you think he still might not get the hint, add a bow tie.

Graduation. Paper that says Congratulations will certainly suffice, though there are graduation papers to be found, if you really want to be specific. It might be more fun, though, to wrap the present in black and add a tassle, making the very box itself resemble a mortarboard. Use school colors if you cannot find black paper. The card? A rolled-up shape, à la sheepskin, of course.

Weddings and anniversaries. Hearts, ribbons, and flowers are the themes; pastels and whites, the colors. Actually, any romantic paper is appropriate and fitting. For wedding showers, use the same papers, or if you prefer, find those printed with raindrops and umbrellas. Baby-shower papers are in a class of their own, the symbols of infancy their adornment.

Christmas. It would take a long list to encompass the myriad symbols found on Christmas wrappings. Many are they; just take your choice. For lovely gifts given during the winter months especially, and for non-churchgoing friends, have general Happy Holiday papers on hand.

Opposite: A balloon may not be your mode of transportation, but Bon Voyage is the message of this special-occasion wrapping.

Other Origins for Originality

By definition, any paper large enough to go around a box is a wrapping paper. Don't shun non-wrapping papers. True, you can always resort to them when you have a present and no decorative paper in the house. But they are not only serviceable. With a little imagination they can become charming and unique wraps, and a most welcome change of pace. The following are just a few thoughts. Look around your home, and add your own.

Newspapers. Choose the section most closely related to the interests of the person who will receive the gift. Or match the section, or newspaper, to the gift. *The Wall Street Journal* is a natural for a book on handling finances, while the real estate section might well cover a housewarming gift. Or try a menu from a foreign restaurant or a colorful foreign newspaper. Who knows—maybe your friend studies Chinese. And remember the comics, especially a favorite strip.

Maps. Large maps—local county maps, geographical maps, nautical maps, road maps, subway maps, world maps, and reproductions of antique maps—will cover some packages ordinary-sized paper cannot without piecing. An obvious choice for a goodbye present. Maps make intriguing wraps. Use their major colors as a cue for the ribbon or tie.

Telephone directories. Now you know what to do with last year's phone book; use it to personalize your presents. With a felt-tip marker to match the ribbon or tie, circle the recipient's name. For popular names circle the entire column!

And still more. Computer print-out paper, old blueprints, wallcovering, shelf paper, and sheet music are all pleasing and potential papers. Experiment!

Opposite: Non-wrapping papers can make the most exotic wraps.

Make Your Own Wrappings

Much like the handmade gift, the personalized gift wrap embodies the true spirit of giving. We have already suggested a number of ways to personalize your gift. The most impressive way is to make your own paper. The process can be as complicated or as simple as you wish. Some papers take great effort and emerge as minor works of art. Others, with little effort, achieve almost the same effect. Whichever method you choose, watching the pattern you created take shape is its own reward.

Start with a good work surface and ample space.

Stamping Papers

Stamps are where you find them, often in the vegetable crisper or fruit bowl.

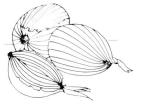

Your basic tools are as close as the greengrocer. Nature provides us with the most natural of stamps—fruits and vegetables. For a stamp with a design cut into it, nothing serves quite so well as a potato. (Slice a raw one in half and cut out a design in it.) For a design with an organic motif, use the lines of cut vegetables. Try green peppers or onions. Allow the vegetable or fruit to dry for a half hour before using it. Another handy stamp is a kitchen sponge. Simply cut it into the desired shape. For stamping you will need water-based acrylic paint, a shallow dish, a strip of waste paper, and shelf or kraft paper, which make excellent backgrounds.

1. Thin down water-based acrylic paint in a shallow dish with a few drops of water until it is finger-paint consistency. Have a strip of waste paper ready.

2. Put the stamp in the paint, stamp off excess paint on the waste paper, and when the amount of paint is right so the color is not too light or dark, start stamping. The richness of color will vary slightly from stamp to stamp and enhance the hand-crafted quality of the finished design.

Opposite: Marbelize your paper, stencil it with footprints, or stamp it using an onion.

Stenciling Paper

A stencil is a thin sheet of metal or paper, in this case acetate paper, perforated in such a way that when paint is applied to the sheet, the designs or letters are marked on the surface beneath. First make a stencil; then use it to stencil on paper.

Today's water-based acrylic paints, which adhere to most papers, including shelf paper, have made stenciling quite simple. Create your own design for the stencil, or trace one from a magazine, cookie cutter, or greeting card. You will need an acetate sheet and a craft knife or sharp razor blade to make the stencil, one tube of water-based acrylic paint for each color you use, a saucer, a brush to mix the paint, a fine sponge for applying the paint, or, as illustrated, a sponge toe cap—really intended for a sore toe (and available in pharmacies), but also perfect to use on your thumb or another finger for stenciling.

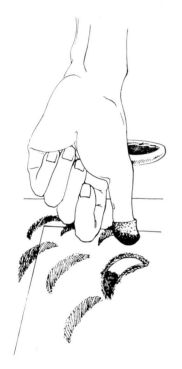

To create a complete design, move your acetate stencil to another part of the paper and repeat the pattern.

1. Thin down water-based acrylic paint in a saucer with a few drops of water until it is the consistency of finger paint. (If you are mixing several colors for a special shade, combine them before thinning with water.)

2. Place the acetate sheet over the pattern you want to stencil and cut out the pattern with a craft knife or sharp razor blade. This patterned sheet of acetate is now your stencil.

3. Put the stencil on the paper. Dip your thumb or finger with the sponge cap on it in the paint. Then dab the paint all over the stencil in an up-and-down motion, rather than spreading it on. Carefully lift the stencil off the paper, so the paint does not smear, and allow painted paper to dry.

Marbelizing Paper

To marbelize paper is to give it the mottled look of marble.

Thanks to spray paint, the technique is now easier than ever. You will need space, clips for hanging wet paper, a place to spray, a deep wide pan, rubber gloves, tongs, water, and rag paper.

Spray paint on water, slip the paper from one end of the pan into the water and draw it up through the sprayed paint.

Part of the fun in marbelizing paper is the element of chance. You can follow the same directions every time and every time your paper will look a little different. So experiment; the magical is never precise.

The key is to work quickly. The paper must be dipped in the paint and removed before it has a chance to dry. Practice with a few sheets of scrap paper. You can select whatever colors you wish, but the lines and swirls you create are in the hands of the gods.

1. Cover a table or work area (4 feet by 4 feet is ample) with newspaper, and place your pan in the center of it. Fill it with water to about 1 inch from the top.

2. Choose two or more colors of oil-based spray paint and keep them handy.

3. Spray your main color on the water, and quickly spray on the other color(s) you are using. We believe four is the limit.

4. Slip the paper rapidly into the pan from one end, so that it goes through the oil paint on the surface and down into the water. Almost at the same time, pull the paper up and across the surface of the paint. Basically you are quickly skimming the paint to make it adhere to the paper. Use tongs if you drop the paper.

5. Hang the marbelized paper to dry.

6. Repeat the process for each sheet. Blot any paint remaining on the water with a tissue. Start with fresh water when necessary.

Piecing and Packing with Paper

If you must piece the paper on the outside of your package, it need not look makeshift. If you must pack the inside, it need not be stuffed with wads of tissue crumpled willy-nilly. Some tips follow:

Piecing

Piecing is necessary when the package to be covered is larger than the paper you have.

If you have to piece, and you are using a patterned paper, overlap the two pieces of paper until the patterns are in line, much as you would do to match wallcovering. Attach the two pieces with double-stick tape in a few places just under the overlap.

1. Use the same technique for two sheets of paper in contrasting colors or patterns. (One sheet will cover the bulk of the package, as in Figure #1. The contrasting sheet acts as an inset.) Turn under a ½-inch hem on both sides of the larger piece to hide its raw edges. It should overlap the contrasting piece by 1 inch on either side. Attach the two pieces with double-stick tape in a few places just under the overlap on both sides.

2. The panel of contrasting paper is now an integral part of the package design. (See Figure #2.)

Packing with Paper

Packing performs two functions. It dresses up the inside of the box, and it secures the gift. Good packing is extremely important for fragile items, of course, and for items you intend to mail. (For tips on packing for mailing, see the last chapter.)

Tissue paper is the basic tool for packing inside the gift box. Use any solid color, or a combination of colors. Printed tissue papers can create the most spectacular interior of all.

Opposite: Grace is not confined to the outside when a box is lined with the flat fold and Japanese fan fold.

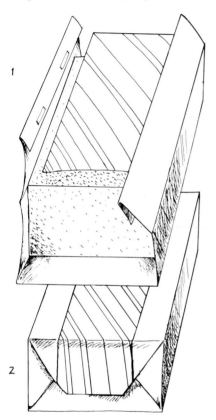

When piecing two sheets of paper contrasting in color or pattern, turn under ½-inch hems on both sides of the larger sheet. Allow 1 inch on either side of the larger sheet for overlapping.

1

2

The flat fold is the basic one used to surround a gift. For articles of clothing or other objects unlikely to slip in a flat rectangular box, it is quick, easy, and the only lining and packing you will probably need. To give it a finished look, follow these steps.

1. Put two sheets of tissue paper one on top of another in a box, with the long ends of the tissue overlapping the sides. To make the paper fit the bottom of the box, it is necessary to make a pleat in the middle of the paper and carefully center the paper, thus reducing the width of the paper to fit just inside the edges of the box. Place the gift in the box. Fold one side of the paper over the gift, then the other.

2. Fold under the raw edge of the top piece of tissue if it overlaps too far, and finger-press it lightly. Attach a decorative seal if desired.

3. If the paper is too short to overlap, grasp each sheet of tissue separately, and pull in opposite directions until there is sufficient paper to cover the gift.

4. To wrap round or squarish presents, first put 2 sheets of tissue paper in the box with the long ends overlapping the *sides*, and fold the tissue paper lengthwise (as in Step #1).

Then:

A. Put another doubled sheet of tissue paper in the box with the tissue's long *ends* overlapping the ends of the box. Fold the center of the tissue paper lengthwise (as in Step #1), so it fits just inside the edges of the box.

B. From the ends, fold one side of the paper over the gift, then the other. Finger-press the fold without sealing. Then fold over the paper from the sides and finish as before.

The Japanese fan fold is the best one to use for packing, as it makes a snug, safe nest in which the present can rest.

With fragile items, you might want a box much larger than the present, as the fan fold will fill the space from top to bottom and side to side and protect the present should it be dropped. Use the Japanese fan fold even when it is not needed to protect the present. It is a clever way to make a gift fit nicely into a box that is actually too large.

Grasp the long ends of the tissue and gather it to you. Form serpent shapes and fit them loosely into the box.

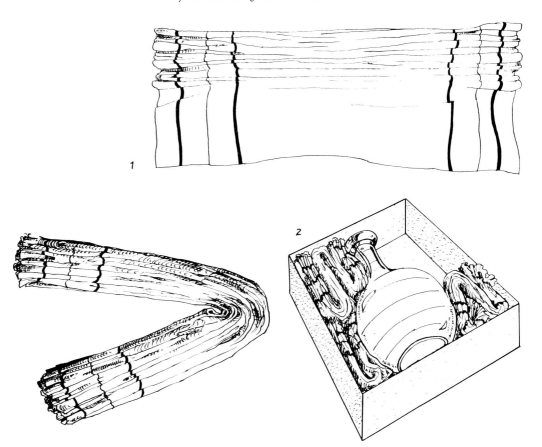

1. Put a piece of tissue paper in front of you lengthwise. Grasp the ends and gather it, forming accordion folds (as in Figure # 1). Leave it loosely bunched so air pockets created along the folds can help buffer the present. Do not press the creases down; the paper should have a springy quality. Place the tissue in the box and cover the bottom with one or more of the bunched tissue forms. The present can now rest upon this springy layer.

2. Place the present in the box. Add more fan folds around the sides and on top for real safety.

A really exquisite ribbon or tie can outshine the paper it surrounds. Any ribbon or tie, no matter how humble, can be made to look lovely, however, if you come to it armed with an arsenal of clever bow techniques. Before you begin, consider these pointers:

Ribbons. They vary in widths and materials. Cloth ribbons can be solid colors, woven in stripes and plaids, or printed with patterns. Some interesting textures are lace, velvet, satin, grosgrain, moire, burlap, and lawn cloth. Wrapping ribbon usually does not match sewing ribbon in quality, which is why it is less expensive.

Synthetic ribbon material. These include metallics and shiny non-woven ones with a satiny finish. Some are self-sticking when moistened with a drop of water. Another popular variation is the ridged narrow ribbon, ideal for crimping.

Stiff ribbons. They lend themselves to the perkiest bows, while the more malleable ribbons are easier to shape and mold into pouffed chrysanthemum bows, for example. All gift-wrapping ribbons must have some stiffness, though, so that bows will remain fresh-looking. The fabric ribbons are frequently stiffened with sizing to give needed starchiness.

Ties. They are the same on all sides and thus are easier to work with than ribbons—which often have a front and back side, or, if you wish, a right and wrong side. Ties are particularly suitable for children's use. A simple knot, child's play, is enough to join the ends.

Opposite: plain and fancy. Clockwise from upper left: circles-in-circles, fuzzy pom-pom, basic bow tie, and chrysanthemum.

Almost all gift-wrap ties are composed of synthetic yarn, primarily acrylic. There are a few polyester and nylon yarn ties. Some synthetic yarn ties stay tautly twisted, even after many uses. Others are easily separated, and are good for making pom-poms or combed-out tassel effects.

A variety of other materials can serve as ties — knitting yarns, scraps of wool, silk thread, plain string, or macrame cord. Try jute, to be found in craft stores in a wide range of colors, or satin or suede cord to dress up a special package.

Color coordinate your ribbons or ties to the paper, using one of the wrap's colors or a contrasting hue. To create a package with visual impact, select a ribbon in either a lighter or darker shade of the paper's color.

Take advantage of the abundance of ribbons and ties and mix-match them. Two-toned bows are doubly effective. Or place a ribbon of one color or pattern along the center of a match-mated one. The only rule of thumb is to use complementary materials — satins with velvets, burlap with simple lawn cloth.

Basic Wrapping Patterns

How you wrap or tie the ribbon around the box will determine the type of bow to be used. Although the crisscrossed ribbon with the bow centered on the box is the most popular pattern, there is no law, even unwritten, that says it must be so.

Try placing the crisscrossed junction off center, either in a corner, or more to one side than the other. Square boxes often look best with centered bows; rectangular boxes with bows off center.

Run the ribbon diagonally over one corner and tie on the opposite corner. This pattern is best on flat boxes, where the ribbon fits snugly around the corners.

Tape ribbons or ties to the back of the package to create a windowpane pattern by bringing some of them over the top and down the length of the package, and others around its width. For an interesting basket weave effect, use different colored ribbons and interweave them on the front of the package.

Around and around they go. Be creative with ribbons.

Wrap a series of ribbons around the package, all going in the same direction. Tape the ends of the ribbon to the back of the package. In the front, pinch the ribbons together in the center of the package, and place a pom-pom bow on top.

When you are working out the overall ribbon pattern, consider bows or any other trimming you plan to add.

The Basic Bow Tie

Let's face it, you cannot do without it. If you can tie a pretty bow, you can fashion a pretty package. And skeptics among you take heed, the basic bow tie is the easiest and fastest one to make. Here is how you can both tie a present and move right into making a beautiful bow.

1. Start by measuring off enough ribbon to make one half of a bow, plus a little extra (1 loop and a short tail). Crimp the ribbon at that point, twisting it in a right angle. Place it on the box where you will want the bow to appear, and hold.

2. Lift the box, slide the ribbon under, and bring it back to where the ribbon is crimped. Pull the ribbon tight, intertwine it with the crimped ribbon, and twist. The ribbon is now wrapped around the package in one direction, with the short end at a right angle.

3. Wrap the remaining ribbon around the package and bring it up to the crimped cross-section. Measure ribbon the same length as the first ribbon end, and cut. Slide the ribbon under the cross-section and tie both ends to make a knot. You are now ready for the basic bow tie.

4. Form 1 ribbon into a loop, making sure its tail is front-side out (it will be on the top).

Bring the other ribbon up, around, and over the first loop, and *loosely* draw it through to form a second loop. You now have a bow. If the bow and ribbon are full enough to cover most of the center, use the inside (back) surface of the bow to make the knot. If they are not full enough, and the back of the ribbon is unattractive, feel free to fiddle, which is why the knot was only loosely tied.

5. Make sure the best side of the first loop's tail end is showing. Twist over the second loop of the bow so its tail will be best side out. (The knot will hold it in position.) Now, turn over half the knot part of the ribbon to cover its bad side. Shorten the loops and pull to secure the knot.

An alternative is to tie the package at the back and add a ready-made bow. To make one, start with ribbon and string such as kite string. Form the ribbon into two loops the width of the bow you want to make. The ends will be crisscrossed. Tie the center with string, or thin wire if you prefer. Cover the center with matching ribbon, doubled over, and secure it with double-stick tape. Leave ends long enough to attach the bow or again use double-stick tape.

Fold the ribbon at a right angle. Bring it around the box and cross. Encircle in the other direction, draw the ribbon under and knot. Make a loop and circle it, with the little circle inside out. Adjust the bow so the front sides of the ribbon show on the tails. Pull the bow tight.

Chrysanthemum Bows (Ribbon Pom-Poms)

If you do not have the time to make your own, rest assured that shiny, ready-made chrysanthemum bows can be found in many gift shops. They are simple to do, though, and can be made in just the right size for the package you have in mind.

1. Form a circle of ribbon that overlaps in the center back, and has a tail 1 inch longer at the overlap. Tape. Flatten the circle and use it as the dimension for the finished bow. (The bow will be slightly smaller, because it will fluff up.) Continue to wrap the ribbon in circles to the desired size of the bow. The larger the bow, the more ribbon to wrap.

2. Finish the outside circle by overlapping it at the same point as the inside overlap. Again leave a 1-inch tail. Tape.

3. Flatten the circles and fold in half so that both sets of loops are at one end.

Cut diagonal wedges off either side of the ribbon's center fold. By cutting in from the outside edge, you are less apt to cut through the center of the ribbon. Allow enough ribbon — at least ¼ inch — so it will not pull apart along the center fold.

4. Tie tightly at the center where you have cut the wedges, with ribbon or kite string. (You can use the same ribbon to attach the bow.)

5. To shape the bow, start with one end and pull out the inside loop to the right, then down, and twist it across the center notch. Pull the next inside loop down to the left and twist.

Alternate sides, pulling out loops from right and left, until that end is complete. Reverse the bow and repeat the process.

6. Fluff into shape. For a two-toned bow, make two bows, one smaller than the other. Place the smaller one on top and tie the bows together.

To make chrysanthemum bows, wrap the ribbon in circles. Flatten. Fold and cut the diagonal wedges. Tie the center. Pull out the loops and fluff the bow.

*Draw the ridged ribbon carefully across
a scissor blade or a dull knife to make a
crinkled ribbon pom-pom.*

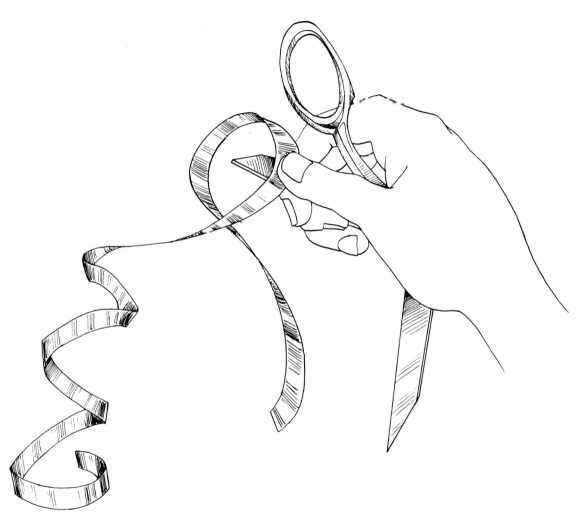

Crinkled Ribbon Pom-Poms

Relax. To make this bow, the ribbon does most of the work. However, only ridged ribbon designed for crimping will do.

Elementary as one, two, three:

Tie a ribbon around the box, leaving about 5-inch ends with which to tie on a bow. You will want enough ribbon, once crimped, to make a chrysanthemum-shaped mound.

To crimp, hold the ribbon tightly in place with your thumb and draw it across a scissor blade or a dull knife.

Intertwine loops of the crinkled ribbon and tie the ribbon to the package. Shake to make certain the loops are secure and tie them with an additional piece of ribbon if necessary. Crimp ends.

You can have more fun with a package simply by using more than one crinkled ribbon pom-pom to adorn it. Try a package with the ribbon's intersection off center, perhaps a good bit to the upper left. Leave enough ribbon to create 2 long streamers. Now, using double-stick tape, attach a large crinkled pom-pom at the ribbon's intersection. Decorate the end of each streamer with a small pom-pom.

So easy and so festive. Give the box a good shake to be sure the pom-pom holds fast.

Circles-in-Circles

This bow is not only artistic, it is versatile. Circles-in-circles can be a flat bow, a standing bow, or a combination. Use ribbon that is attractive on both sides, as they will both show. Vary the colors or work with only one. Small circles can be linked with larger ones to create intriguing forms and to further the harmony of a package's shape.

1. Curl a ribbon around your finger and secure it where it overlaps. For regular ribbon, use double-stick tape; self-stick ribbon need only be moistened.

2. Continue wrapping the ribbon in increasingly larger circles, keeping it in line with the original circle. Anchor each circle at the spot you anchored the first. Finish one circle-in-circle and repeat the process until you have as many as you wish.

3. To attach 2 finished circles of self-sticking ribbon, place them back to back, moisten the surfaces, and press together. (If the ribbon is not self-sticking, glue circles together or use double-stick tape. Attach finished circles to each other one at a time.)

To attach the bow to a package, weave a ribbon of whatever length you need through the main center of the composed bow. Tie it just in back of the bow, and tie it again to the package ribbon.

Fuzzy Pom-Poms

The principle for making fuzzy pom-poms remains the same, even though the effects vary enormously depending on the material used. Small versions of the pom-pom can be transformed into charming, fanciful animals by adding bits of felt for hands and feet, and dots for eyes. Medium and large-sized fuzzy pom-poms are a natural finish to ties of matching yarn.

Use any yarn that has plushy ends, such as acrylic yarn giftwrap ties, macrame cord, and knitting yarns, both synthetic and wool. Make multicolored fuzzy pom-poms by combining odds and ends, thus using up your old scraps at the same time.

1. Cut out matching cardboard circles, each with a hole in the center and a slit wide enough to slide the yarn through.

1

2

3

With this bow, the more you go in circles, the more glorious the effects.

Cut out two cardboard circles. Wind the yarn around them. Cut the yarn on the outside edge. Tie around the middle. Remove the cardboard. Fluff out the pom-pom, and steam if needed.

2. Place cardboard circles together and wrap yarn around them from the center to the edge until the cardboard surface is covered.

3. Slide scissors between the two cardboard wheels and cut the yarn just on the outside perimeter.

4. When the yarn is cut, slide a length of yarn between the two cardboards with extra length for attaching, and tie a firm knot around the center of all the cut yarns.

5. Cut off the cardboards. Fluff the ball by hand or steam over a steam iron for extra fluffiness.

Flourishes are your signature. They give a package its final touch of individuality and fix you as a creative and thoughtful gift wrapper.

Special flourishes can be found in gift stores and are frequently designed to coordinate with specific papers or represent a special occasion. What wedding cake would be complete without the bride and groom smiling out from its top?

You need not look far to discover flourishes. You need only know where to look. Some can be unearthed in office supply stores. Others are from the paper department, the kitchen, or the glitter section of the craft store. Add to these the inventive things you can do with fabric, as an alternative to wrapping paper, and no one will ever accuse you of repeating yourself.

Flourishes can range in price from the very expensive, in which case they are gifts in themselves, to mere pennies. What matters is how they enhance the overall look of the package and spirit of the gift. Some good ways to attach flourishes follow:

1. Glue or tape them. A number of glues available are perfect for the job. White all-purpose glue, which dries clear, works well to attach paper and other fairly light objects with smooth surfaces; super-strength glue that dries in just a few minutes and sticks to practically anything works well for heavier objects and those without flat surfaces. Although these two glues are preferred, almost any household glue will come in handy. You can also attach flourishes with double-stick tape, of course.

Preceding pages: A potpourri of flourishes from here, there, and everywhere.

2. Tie them. Nuts and small pine cones, as examples, need to be tied. To do so, wrap kite string or extremely thin wire (both almost invisible) around them and tie the wire or kite string to the package's ribbon. Or place a dot of super-strength glue on the back of the flourish (an acorn is illustrated), adhere the wire to the glue, and top it with a small piece of paper to seal the bond.

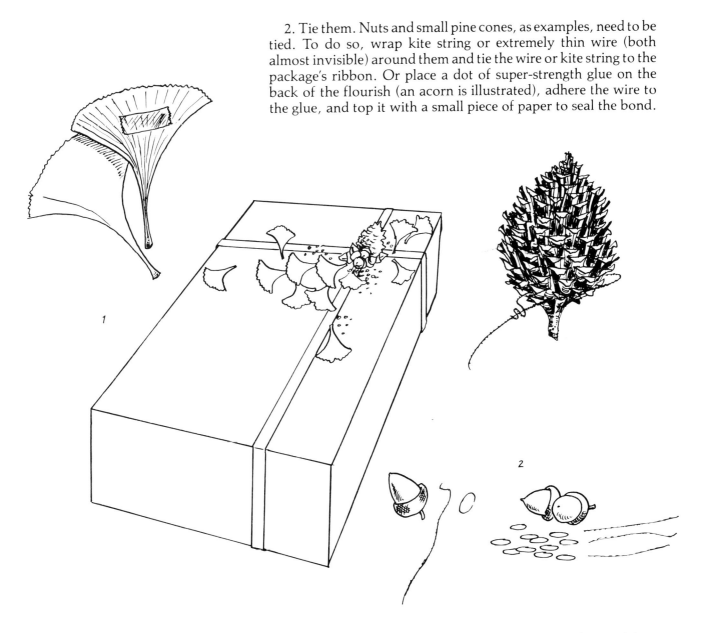

To attach flourishes, wrap wire around them, or glue wire to them, and tie them to the package. Some need only be taped or glued into place.

Natural Accents

Nature does indeed prove endlessly bountiful.

Any time of the year is a good time to collect natural accents, many of which keep in storage, ever ready to dress up a present.

Natural accents bear special meaning. A flourish found on a walk with a friend is a lovely reminder of that moment, when it appears on a gift for that friend. Your imagination is your best guide, but here are some additional thoughts:

Feathers. From the blue jay feather discovered in the woods to the haircomb ornament seen in a fashionable boutique, feathers make delightful flourishes. Slip a single one under a present's bow. Or attach it to a comb or pin backing, making it not only decorative but wearable. To give the feather a finished look, wrap the base with colored tape.

Shells. Today exotic shells command exotic prices, but as any beachcomber will tell you, the best are free. Before using shells as flourishes, scrub them well with clorox and water, allow to dry, and varnish them to bring out the color. (Any clear varnish will do.) Employ super-strength glue to attach a shell to string or wire; or drill a hole in it and hang it on macrame cord to make a pendant. Shells are simple to attach to packages: Adhere large ones to matching wide ribbon with double-stick tape, or use the self-sticking wall hangers designed for hanging pictures.

Flora. All manner of flora make interesting flourishes. Attach leaves directly to the wrapping with double-stick tape. Highlight nuts, such as acorns, with rub-on gold or silver (a waxlike substance, available in craft stores). Combine with tiny pine cones, glue wires to their backs, and gather the wires into one cluster. Tuck dried weeds or flowers through bows. For fresh flowers, wrap the stems in damp paper towels and cover them with aluminum foil and florist's tape before adding to a bow.

Opposite: Feathers, nuts, leaves, and flowers give life to this still life.

From the Office

If you think an office is only a place where work is performed, think again. It is also a veritable gold mine for flourishes. Stock up on wares from the stationery or office supply store and use them to bedeck just about anyone's gift. After all, who among us would not be grateful for a sharpened pencil.

Writing instruments. They make handsome flourishes. Look for brilliant colors in felt-tip markers, pencils, and crayons. If you are one of foresight, order pencils stamped with the person's name. If not, add a cluster of them in the recipient's favorite color. Novelty pens in the shapes of lollipops and candy canes, and even nails, are another alternative. And then there is that old-fashioned pen that actually takes ink. One, as a flourish, is a gift in itself.

Stick-ons. Normally used for color coding, they are marvelous tools with which to create your own designs. Collect them in all sizes, colors, and shapes, and mix with colored tape. Some of the shapes include signals, circles, and rectangles with nicely rounded corners. They show best when on a solid background. A logical use for a large self-sticking label is as a gift tag, as it is meant to be written on anyway. Or play to your heart's content and spell out to whom, and from whom, in self-sticking and brightly colored plastic letters. If you get carried away, all the better. Compose whole sentences. But be certain, if you tend to be wordy, that your box is big enough.

Desk-top accessories. Still more gift-wrapping finds. Attach paper clips and rulers in bright, bold plastic to your presents with double-stick tape. Good-looking memo pads, bookmarks, or an extension cord are just a few of many other possibilities. Whichever you choose, rest assured not all of your creation will end up in the wastebasket.

Opposite: Tools of the office put to work as flourishes.

From the Kitchen

We know that high on the list of favorite gifts is the home-cooked one. But why not take it one step beyond and decorate the container with its ingredients. Cooks will be enchanted with flourishes they can blend, chop, purée, or pound. Look to your larder and, this time, permit a raid on the icebox.

Pasta. Use its multitude of plain and fancy shapes in their uncooked form. Alphabet letters can spell out a message. Attach them with glue and position with tweezers. To enliven pasta shapes, dip them in water tinted with food dye and set on paper towels to dry. Double-dip to intensify the color. Use super-strength glue to attach directly to the ribbon or wrapping paper.

Herbs and spices. For the package that smells as good as it looks, use a handful of home-grown tarragon, or try an aromatic spice like bay leaves or cinnamon sticks. If you intend them to be used, tie them on. Otherwise use double-stick tape.

Utilitarian objects. If it is charitable to find beauty in the most humble, start with the dishcloth and move on to the pot scrubber! Make a lamb with a pot scrubber for its body, and black licorice sticks for its legs. Snip off pieces of licorice to create ears and a nose, and use cake decoration for the eyes. Or try a deer. Use a sponge for the body, popsicle sticks for the legs, and plastic cocktail forks for the antlers. Other possibilities include wooden spoons, and cookie cutters, which can be chosen to fit the occasion — a gingerbread man for Christmas, a bunny for Easter. And do not bypass cake-testing straws, or the many other potential utensils.

Paper goods. Not only are drinking straws the basis for quilling, a craft hobby, they dress up presents in fabulous ways. Use macrame knots to invent forms or just glue them on in linear designs, for pinwheels or plaids.

Opposite: A groaning board of kitchen garnishes: dyed pastas, pot scrubbers, and cinnamon sticks.

Flourishes from Paper

Some of the least expensive flourishes for gifts depend upon paper itself. A paper decoration can do wonders, and cost no more than pennies. And should there be an artist buried in you — even if not — try drawing directly on the paper. A few other suggestions follow:

Doilies. Lacy, frilly, romantic doilies come in white, colors, silver and gold, and are available in a wide range of sizes. Cut them to make star flake designs, or use them as the circles they are. To create fans and collars, pleat doilies by folding them over and over into smaller wedges. Cut along one fold. Glue two or more doilies together to achieve the fullness you need. Make two decorations at the same time by placing a doily on paper and then spray-painting. You will have a colored doily to use as a flourish as well as paper embellished with the doily outline to use as wrapping.

Draw-on designs. All you need is imagination. The wrapping paper is a blank canvas, and you are a painter. Draw, draw, draw. No need to bother with a bow and gift tag. Draw them on. Or tip your hand and sketch what is inside the box. If you are not Van Gogh, remember the children. They are seldom as inhibited as their elders. Supply them with felt-tip markers and put the package in front of them.

Paper flower. Cut 4 strips of wrapping paper. (Use more strips for a larger flower.) Overlap the ends of each strip to form a loop that looks like a shirt collar, and secure the ends with transparent tape. Attach the loops to one another in a flower shape with glue or double-stick tape. Position the flower on the package and secure it with double-stick tape. Decorate the flower's center with a small stick-on or a gummed star. For a gladiola effect, line up the loops in a row.

Decoupage. Use labels from cans, seed packets, magazine cut-outs, or whatever strikes your fancy. Rubber cement is the best material for mounting them on wrapping paper.

Opposite: A white doily with silver-paper center echoes the pattern of the paper.

To Add Glamour

All that glitters may not be gold, but it can be just as bewitching. The gift, swathed in rich paper, beribboned and bedecked with sparkle, casts its spell. The more gussied up, the more glamorous. Or perhaps you like a subtle gleam. In either case, there are softly glowing metallic papers to use as well as brilliant ones with mirror-like surfaces. Add flourishes and each package becomes a star fit for center stage.

Glitter. Children love to add glitter to presents; it's simple, and the results are magical. Most glitter is sold in colors, with or without its own glue. If it is not included, use white all-purpose glue. Wrap the presents. Dribble on glue in free-form lines, shake glitter over them, and allow to dry. Shake off excess glitter. Do one gluing and one color application at a time. Another, more stylized approach is to write names or messages in glue and sprinkle with glitter. Or use stencils to create glittery shapes.

Stick-ons. Notary seals and metallic letters, colored stars, and the gold ones we knew in school, all make pretty decorations. Some are self-sticking, others need a dab of glue to properly adhere to metallic or shiny paper. Work out your design first by positioning the unglued stick-ons. Then lift each one and attach it permanently.

Sewing-box finds. Strung or unstrung, sequins make fabulous additions. Sew or glue them on, as the case may be. For a giddy decoration that is also a gift, use them to adorn a comb, a pen, or any other inexpensive item.

Sweet glitters. They may look like nuggets of gold or silver, but they are really candies and cake decorations in sparkling foil. A tasty, if deceptive, decoration. Use super-strength adhesive to attach them to one another and to the wrapping paper.

Opposite: Create a dramatic accent with chocolate nuggets in foil, clustered as glittering grapes.

Fabric Fancies

Forget paper for the moment and think cloth. It opens up an entirely new range of potential gift wraps.

Nothing could be prettier in spring than flower prints or gossamer pastels. A whisper of yellow or pink chiffon is perfect for that tiny Easter gift. And imagine the richly festive effect of red or green velveteen for a holiday gift, adorned, perhaps, with a sprig of holly.

For a permanent cover, you will probably want just the right fabric for the person to whom you are giving the gift. As most wraps take very little fabric, none of these covers need be costly. And most can be done by hand or machine, with little effort. Cover a box, tie up a gift, bag it, or make a book cover. These are all lovely fabric fancies.

Fabric-Covered Box

The technique for covering a box with fabric is similar to that for covering one with paper (pages 18-20), with one time-saving difference. You can use spray-on adhesive, available in craft stores, to adhere the fabric and give the box a truly professional look. Once the fabric has been applied, cover seams with a coordinated ribbon or fancy trim to ornament it even further. Then spray with fabric protector to keep the surface soil-resistant.

To cover a square box, cut out the fabric following the directions for covering a box with paper. Spray the lid with adhesive and stick it down on the fabric, making sure the lid is centered. Press the fabric onto the box, bring the sides up, and fold them over and into the lid. If necessary, use white all-purpose glue to adhere the fabric securely on the seams. Repeat the steps for the box bottom.

To cover a round box or cookie tin, cut the material to size and use the directions for covering with paper as a general guide (pages 18-20). Spray adhesive on the box and press the fabric into position. Finish the edges with ribbon.

Opposite: A gift of cookies is made sweeter still when its tin is covered with fabric.

Tied Fabric Wraps

For a happy hobo look, wrap a gift in bandannas. For a more sophisticated one, try a silk scarf or a provicial print. You can use ready-made scarves and handerchiefs for these coverings, or cut squares to fit. Finish fabric hems by pinking or rolling them. When it is for show only, glue the roll. Run a thin line of white all-purpose glue along the fabric edge, roll the fabric over the glue, and allow it to dry.

The fold covering is easy.

1. Place the box diagonally on the fabric, and tie 2 opposite ends over it.

2. Tie the remaining 2 ends tightly over the box. Turn all the ends right side out and arrange them decoratively over the box — one bandanna corner draped over each box corner.

3. To make a hobo tote, place the box diagonally on the fabric square and tie the opposite ends. Tuck the ends down over the exposed sides of the box to conceal it completely. Bring up the remaining fabric corners and tie them in a square knot near the tips, creating a handle.

Fabric Book Cover

Transform a commonplace address book into a lasting present with a handsome fabric cover. For the paperback addict, a unique gift is several books each enveloped in a handmade cover. Because the covers can be removed and cleaned, they will last through years of use.

Measure a closed book from the front edge of the book cover, around the back, to the edge of the back cover; add 7 inches (3 inches each for front and back "pockets," and another 1 inch for ½-inch turned hems front and back).

Measure from the top to the bottom edge of the front cover for depth, and add a minimum ½ inch for ¼-inch seam allowances top and bottom. For larger books, increase to 1 inch with ½-inch seam allowances.

Tie opposite corners of the fabric over the box. For a flat box, tie the remaining two corners tight. Arrange the fabric corners flat over the box. For a hobo tote, tie the last two corners near the tips in a square knot, making a handle.

Fit end pockets to the book by wrapping it around the covers, wrong side out, and pinning. Stitch the pockets.
Turn right side out and add a bookmark ribbon.

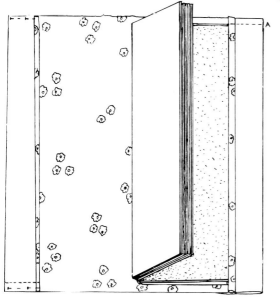

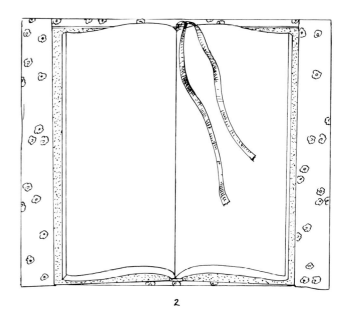

1

2

Cut out the fabric, turn under ½-inch hems on "pockets," and stitch.

1. To make a hidden seam, place the fabric, with its wrong side out, around a closed book. Wrap the ends around the front and back covers, and pin in place.

2. Remove the book and stitch the pocket extensions to the covers (A). Trim hem on the pocket extensions if necessary.

3. Turn the pockets right side out. Press ¼-inch seam allowances (top and bottom), as well as end pockets. Make certain the book fits. Remove the book.
Fold the fabric cover in half, pockets on the outside, and mark both the top and bottom. Tack the hem in place at the bottom. To add a built-in bookmark to the cover, stitch a ribbon, doubled over, to the center top. Cut ribbon bookmarks to the length you wish.

Fabric Bags

Make these in almost any size and in any fabric heavy enough to conceal the contents. Some choices are gingham, calico, velveteen, burlap, cottons of all kinds, and even silks. If you have remnants, here is another time to put them to good use.

Measure the height and circumference of the gift to go into the bag. Measure the fabric and be sure to allow some extra for the bag to go around the item — how much depends upon the thickness of the fabric. Allow sufficient height so that the bag covers the gift and *can easily be drawn closed.* Make the bag pattern.

Stitch both side seams below the casing. Turn under the casing ends and overcast stitch. Fold the casing over ½ inch below the clips and stitch. Thread two ribbons through the casing. Pull taut to close.

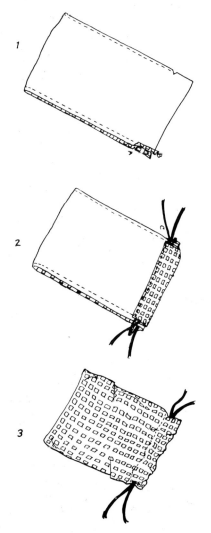

1. Double the fabric, right sides together, and cut to the required width, allowing ½ inch on each side for seams (1 inch total). Cut to the required length, allowing at the top of the fabric ½ inch for a hem, and a minimum of 1 inch for the casing. Make the casing the width of the ribbon plus ½ inch for stitching. Add this length to the total bag height.

From the top of the bag, measure down the width of casing allowance, plus ½-inch hem allowance, and clip (A).

Measure from the top of the fabric double the width of casing allowance plus ½-inch hem allowance. (If the casing is to be 1 inch, allow 2½ inches.) Pin the side seams. Stitch the side seams up to the clip.

Turn under the ends of the casing and overcast stitch along the ends (B).

2. Fold casing over ½ inch below clips. Stitch along this line (C).

3. Turn the bag right side out. Tack the sides of the casing together at the top. Thread two ribbons through the casing slits, one right to left, the other reversed. Pull to close.

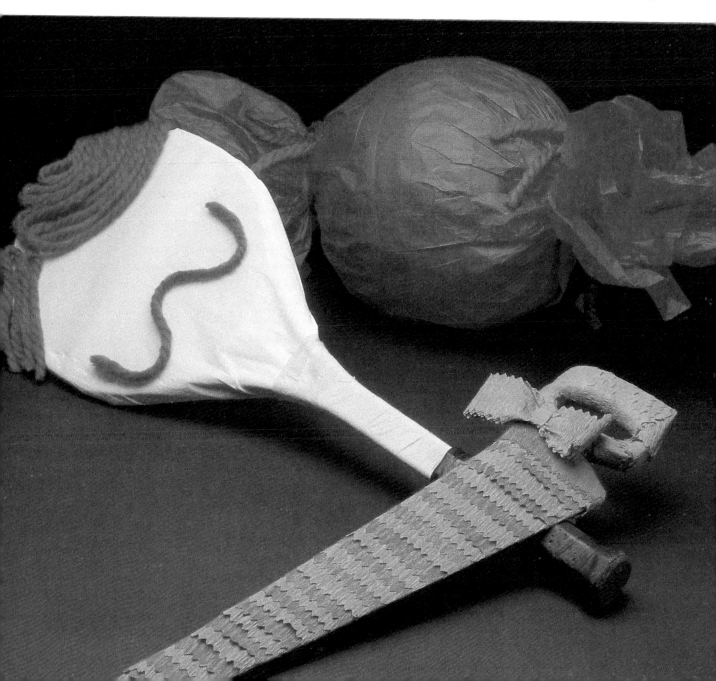

Some presents simply cannot be boxed, at least in a conventional manner. The outsized, for instance. Others you may not *choose* to box, particularly when half the fun is to let the gift's shape give away what is inside. And then there are the times when you just have no boxes on hand. Below are some ways to wrap gifts unboxed:

Use crepe paper. It is very flexible and will stretch to conform to the shape of the object. Decorate the surface any way you wish.

Use crepe paper streamers on long thin objects. Begin by taping two streamers in position, one slightly above and overlapping the other. Try two colors for a zebra stripe effect. Wind the streamers around the object, making sure both colors show with each successive turn, and stretching them to conform to the gift's shape. A single color is good for accents.

Use tissue paper. Make a big, puffy snapper wrap package with tissue paper. Tie off both ends and stand the present on end, if you like.

Make a cornucopia.

1. Start with a sheet of cardboard and draw and cut out wedges, 3 for a three-sided cornucopia, 4 for a four-sided one. (To make economical use of the cardboard, draw the wedges going in different directions.)

Preceding page: The tennis racket, basketball, and handsaw are wrapped to give their secrets away.

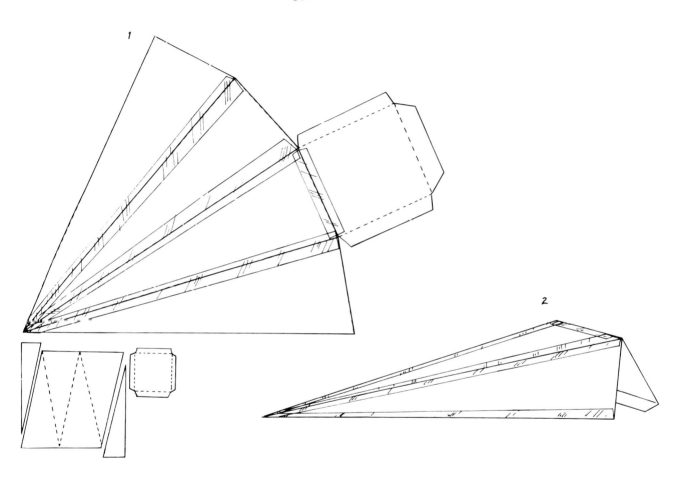

2. Use transparent tape or one of a heavier weight, such as packing tape, to adhere the wedge sides to one another. Cut a top in either a triangle (for the three-sided cornucopia) or a square, making scored flaps on all sides. Miter flap corners. As the cornucopia will be wrapped, the lid can be attached with tape on the outside. Fold the flaps in to close.

It would be an act of profanity to put your cherished home-made brownies in just any old box. Some gifts insist on containers that are almost as good as they are. In this case the package is part of the present, when the brownies are given in a marvelous English cookie tin resembling a double-decker bus.

All of us know that moment when we spot the small thing that reminds us of one particular person. It may not be significant enough to give as a gift, but could be a perfect token to add on to one. Or to use in the actual wrapping. For instance, a unique way to tie a package is to lace it, with shoelaces of course. (See the shoe box on page 81.)

Wrap paper over the box lid, then wrap a contrasting piece around the entire box, leaving a gap down the front of the lid. Double back the edges of the overlapping paper at least 1 inch on each side. Punch holes in the doubled paper and run shoelaces through them.

Gifts on the outside mean extra fun for children. A miniature auto, tucked into or under the bow on a package, is sure to delight a small boy. And what little girl would not love a set of miniature coloring pencils in their own transparent satchel? They are tiny enough to decorate a ribbon.

A special container or add-on may make a present distinctive, but it does not eliminate the need for a gift tag. At any gathering where there is much exchanging of gifts, be it an engagement shower or birthday party, the tag is a thoughtful way of helping everyone remember what came from whom. At times, the tag is the only way someone knows you sent the gift. So have gift tags on hand, or be prepared to make some.

Preceding pages: Two gifts in one. Sometimes even three.

Handsome Gift Containers

In the language of gift wrapping, a container is almost anything attractive that can hold something. Special containers are always welcome and, as we have noted, particularly appropriate for some gifts. So if you are bereft of boxes or wrapping paper at the last minute, look around your house for a usable container. Here are some thoughts:

Baskets. They need no explanation. Oriental stores stock dozens of inexpensive ones, and they are often available through mail-order catalogues. Fill them with colorful tissue to hide the gift, and give open-weave baskets a showy color. And do not overlook their humble country cousins, which a friendly grocer might part with for nothing. Wood-slat mushroom and apple baskets have innate charm and can be used just as they are. If you want to brighten them, however, spray them with paint or apply a wood stain. Do the same with strawberry baskets. Plastic vegetable containers, by the way, resemble wicker when sprayed with white paint.

See-throughs. Fish bowls, brandy snifters, cannisters, and vases are among the glass containers most handy for gifts.

Again, stuff them with colored tissue. Create pop art with a tall soda glass: tissue for a strawberry soda, crimped ribbon for bubbles, a ball for a cherry, and the obligatory straw.

Plastics make good see-through containers as well — perhaps a birdhouse, breadbox, or even a storage closet container. The obvious, of course, are the small cubes, abundant either in colors or clear.

Clever go-togethers. A colander for homemade pasta; new pajamas inside a pillowcase; a salad spinner for spices, vinegar, and gourmet oil; crayons and clips in a drawer organizer; an In-and-Out basket to hold personalized stationery; a tote in which to carry a warm-up suit; a miniature trunk for a new doll; a covered bin for a collection of balls in all sizes. And on, and on. The options are endless.

Give beautiful apples in an all-purpose basket bedecked with a ribbon.

Gift Add-Ons

Who among us has not earned a bonus? How nice then to find one right in sight, on the outside of a package, and to know that it will serve long after its perishable mate has been scrapped. Add-ons can be pricey, or cost mere pennies. Here are some suggestions to fit just about any mood and pocketbook:

For Women

Decorate haircombs, barrettes, or bobby pins, and clamp them on the package's ribbon.

Make sachets from scraps of fabric and lace by stitching miniature squares stuffed with perfume-scented cotton or soap.

Treat an elastic headband or elastic sports belt as a ribbon and wind it around the gift.

Wrap the present in a handkerchief or scarf.

Tie a pair of embroidery scissors onto the bow, or stick knitting needles into a yarn pom-pom.

Attach a purse-sized flask of her favorite perfume.

Secure the ribbon with a scarf clasp or attach a stickpin to the ribbon.

Tuck in a kitchen gadget — melon baller, cake-testing straws, or a set of cocktail picks.

For Men

Put a new pocket diary under the bow of a Christmas present.

Use a novelty soap on a rope as a tie.

Add seed packets to the gardener's gift.

For an athlete, string wristbands on the gift's ribbon.

Or, for the jogger, hang a pedometer from the ribbon.

Poke a fishhook in a cork and center it on the bow.

Tie the box with a heavy-duty extension cord.

Tie on a really good corkscrew.

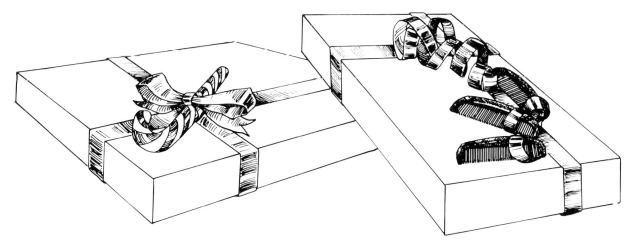

For Children

Sweeten the present with a jumbo candy bar.

Tie an eight-year-old's present with a jump rope.

Attach a jackknife to a camper's present.

Add crayons, pencils, felt-tip markers, novelty erasers, and a box of personal self-stick stars.

Give a teenager a telephone/address book tucked under the ribbon.

General Suggestions

A box of bookplates inside the gift and one on the outside as a seal.

If nothing will make them stop smoking, give in; string stylish matchboxes on the ribbon.

A miniature flashlight under the bow.

Earmuffs wrapped around a box, hugging each side. Draw a face on the wrapping paper, which should be plain, and make hair with yarn tie for the top.

Gift Tags and Cards

Gift tags can work in two ways on a package; they can play a dominant role in its design, or they can be so subtle you really do not see them until you look closely.

Either way, you will want to use some kind of tag or card on each gift, if only for purposes of identification. But if the tag or card is large enough, it also offers a good chance to say something special to commemorate the occasion.

Spectacular gift cards. To no one's surprise, they abound in gift shops. Some can be bought to match wrapping paper, while others are so appropriate they ask to be left out of their envelopes and used on a gift as its center attraction.

Gift tags that are gifts. Great fun to collect. Look for objects on which you can put a label for your message. Novelty key rings — monogrammed or not — are good choices. So too are giant flat lollipops, bookmarks, or a fancy fan. Open the fan to decorate a large package, and lightly tape your message to the back. Or slip what you want to say inside a luggage tag. And if you really mean to impress, give the inveterate traveler a luggage tag imprinted with his or her name; do the same with a toothbrush for a child. Use a printer's block initial or a monogrammed handkerchief. Tuck the message underneath the monogrammed corner and display the initial proudly.

Money-saving gift tags. A simple and classic one can be made with a lovely piece of wrapping paper; glue it on a rectangular piece of white paper to serve as a backing, fold it in half, and voilà, a gift tag. There are all manner of packaged stick-ons at your disposal, from labels to decorative seals. Or cut out and glue on what appeals to you, be it a magazine picture or a can label. And last, if you are even-tempered and dexterous, carefully pick out the fortune in a fortune cookie, write your wish, and put it back in.

Opposite: A shell lettered with a felt-tip marker is a pretty tag for summer. A cracker lettered with cake decoration is an edible one for the hungry.

Last-Minute Gifts

If you are of a mind to think ahead, chances are you have them. If you are like many of us, you don't. *They* are those last-minute presents, of course, on hand to give when we least expect to. There is nothing quite so awkward as having a gift for everyone at a holiday gathering except the unexpected guest. It is the better part of wisdom, then, to stock a few presents that can be quickly unveiled. You can rest easy, knowing you are prepared to rise to any last-minute occasion. (To protect gifts from dust, store them in plastic bags.)

Here are a few pointers for stocking up:

Keep some non-perishable gifts: a covered book with blank pages for personal notes, particularly handsome pens, a pocket astrology guide, elegant soaps, assorted charms for a bracelet, a boot shoehorn, or an adult puzzle. For men and women, stationery is always welcome, as are desk accessories; a letter opener, for instance, a fancy stamp holder, a stapler or tape dispenser. Large candles, perhaps with an inexpensive candle holder, are also good, but remember scented ones lose their fragrance with time.

Children are never a problem: jigsaw puzzles, stuffed toys, decks of cards, magic sets, scarves, folk toys, diaries that lock, coloring books, crayons, and almost anything miniature.

Appeal to the hidden sybarite in your friends: a tin of crackers and gourmet jams in a breakfast basket; imported mustards, oils, and vinegars; rich chocolates, or dried fruits. Tea sampler sets, spices from faraway places, and a delicate garnish like sugared violets. Fresh fancy fruits, carefully selected, need only a bowl or basket for a finish.

For the cook, there are always dish towels, potholders, and special knives, but why not such a charming bit of esoterica as a strawberry huller.

Opposite: It may be presented at the last minute, but stock the gift with a long shelf life.

At least the paper companies have taken some of the drudgery out of the task, by offering all the materials you will need. So arm yourself with a good supply of tapes, kraft paper, non-stretching twine, extra cardboard, sturdy boxes to use as mailing cartons, and mailing labels. Do not skimp. If presents are wrapped improperly for mailing, even the best gift wrap in the world will not hold up, to say nothing of the gift.

Regulations

Ask your local conveyers for up-to-date information and restrictions on packages. New materials are frequently introduced to make wrapping easier, but are acceptable only to some carriers, not all. Shiny tough plastic tape, for instance, may be all right with United Parcel Service and the local bus line, but rejected by the post office because stamps do not adhere to it. Check the overall dimensions and weight of your packages with the carriers as well. Do this first, as the way you wrap could be determined by which carrier you will use. Main post offices have booklets giving you the latest postal regulations; other carriers can be queried by phone.

Once you have decided how the package is to be sent, there are useful packing techniques to ensure your gift's safe arrival.

Opposite: Festive mailing paper takes over for its plain Jane cousin.

Recycle your box by turning it inside out. Save on wrapping by labeling directly on the clean surface.

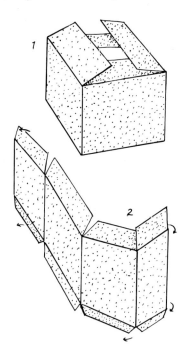

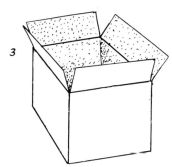

Making Boxes

Start with a sturdy box large enough to hold the gift with extra room on all four sides. Fill in the space with packing to create a buffer between the gift and the outside walls of the box.

To make a mailing container, one of the best tricks around is to turn a box inside out. This is how to do it most efficiently:

1. Choose a box with top and bottom flaps completely intact. Carefully slit the tape with a knife or scissors, to open the bottom flaps. Trim any excess tape.

2. Slit the length of the box at one corner, to open it completely. Turn the box inside out.

3. Using extra-strong tape — reinforced craft tape with filament threads is probably most acceptable to the post office — retape the corner with the inside surface now on the outside.

Tape the bottom into its original configuration. Tape the two side flaps first, then the outer flaps. Seal the opening between these two flaps and along the edges where the flap ends are exposed, to avoid their being ripped in the mail.

4. Pack the box and tape the top closed. Reinforce with cord.

Packing Inside

Crumpled newspaper remains the most universal packing material. Put it on the bottom, sides, and top of the gift package, shake the box, and add more if the package rattles.

For very fragile gifts, put them in a second inner box filled with more paper, or popcorn, a good small-volume packing material. Seal inner box before packing.

For more than one gift or a very heavy one, make compartments and reinforcements from pieces of cardboard. (Partitions keep a heavy package centered in the carton, and prevent several gifts in the same carton from crushing each other.)

Cut slits in the cardboard and interweave it, liquor-carton fashion. Better yet, get liquor cartons and shape the divisions to your needs.

All-Purpose Packing Knot

If you learn to tie only one knot in your life, this should be the one. Once you have mastered it, you can securely tie any carton. It is a clove hitch variation.

1. Tie a knot in the cord end. Wrap the cord around the package, and entwine so that the long end is at a right angle and the short knotted end doubles back on itself.

2. Bring the short cord over itself, forming a loop.

3. Double the cord back under itself and up through the loop. Draw it tight. You now have a knot known as a half hitch.

4. Repeat the same motions: Form a loop, bring the end under the stable part of cord, up through the loop, and draw it tight.

5. Wrap the loose cord around the box in a perpendicular direction. Cut, leaving enough cord for another half hitch. Tie the cord on the opposite side of the first knot. Draw the finished knot tight.

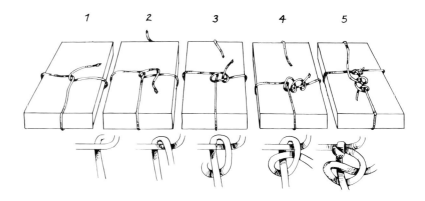

Make a noose to go around the package in one direction, using a half hitch knot. Draw the cord around the box in the other direction, allowing enough for another half hitch. Cut. Tie the cord on the opposite side of the knot.

Acknowledgments

We are grateful to the following manufacturers for the use of their fine products in the preceding pages:

American Greetings Corp., 30, 38, 46, 58-59, 62, 66, 77

Con-Tac, Vinyl by Comark Plastics Division — United Merchants and Manufacturers, Inc., 17

Family Line Company, 8, 29, 58-59

Finch Handprints, Division of Nigel Quinney, 33

Gaylord Specialties Corp., 21, 43, 80-81

C. R. Gibson Company, 33

Gift Box Corporation of America, folded boxes throughout

Gordon Fraser Gallery, Ltd., 21

Hallmark, 24, 46, 58-59, 69, 77, 80-81, 90

Handi-Wipe, 66

Krylon Spray Paint, 38

Stephen Lawrence Co., 2, 8. 58-59, 62, 65, 66, 80-81

Lion Ribbon Co., 2, 17, 30, 33, 37, 46, 58-59, 62, 65, 66, 70, 73, 86, 89

Norcross, Inc., 27, 29, 34, 46, 62, 65, 70, 80-81, 86

Paper Moon Graphics Co., 34

3-M, Scotch Tape, Scotch Craft Mount, Scotch Super-Strength Glue

Index